Hopsalot's Garden

by Kimberly Weinberger

SCHOLASTIC INC.
New York Toronto London Auckland Sydney
Mexico City New Delhi Hong Kong

Spring is the time
to plant and to grow.
Hopsalot the Rabbit
knew just where to go.

"My garden!" he said.

"It will grow **big** and **tall**."

So he got out his seeds.

Then he planted them all.

Summer soon came
but Hopsalot frowned.
His leaves were so **short**
and close to the ground.

Hopsalot's friends
could not tell him why
his garden grew **low**
instead of **high**.

Kisha had planted her seeds
the same way.

"And look!" she said.

"See what I picked today."

Casey showed off

his tomato so red.

"It's **bigger** than Kisha's flower," he said.

Hopsalot sighed.

Tomatoes and flowers!

He had only leaves,

through sun and rain showers.

"I think that your garden
may be a bit slow.
Just wait," said Eleanor.
"In time it will grow."

Frankie stopped by

with corn that grew **tall**.

Pierre had strawberries

so sweet and so **small**.

Edison brought lettuce
that was green, **round**, and **fat**.

CJ's orange pumpkin was
even **bigger** than that!

Hopsalot thought,

All their gardens are great!

Big and **tall**, **short** and **fat** —

but I must still wait.

Then it was fall.

A cool wind blew.

Hopsalot smiled.

"Now I know what I grew!"

With a pull and a tug,

Hopsalot gave a shout.

"Come and take a look!"

Then a carrot popped out.

Hopsalot smiled
as he took a big bite.
"Not too **big** or too **small**,"
he said. "It's just right!"